ABUZZ

VERY AMERICAN POETRY[26+]

Robert E. Ray

For my mother and father,
Georgia & Marvin Ray

In everything give thanks.

—Paul the Apostle

After this I looked, and there before me was a *great multitude* that no one could count, from every nation, tribe, people and language, standing before the throne and before the Lamb. They were wearing white robes and were holding palm branches in their hands.

—Revelation 7:9

The Scrum

Kentucky, circa 1930

J ames lolls in the cafe, back to the wall.
 The waitress brings warm bread in a pawned pyx;
not local pottery, nacre knob, pearl
plucked from the Atlantic, ceramics
the pyx and mug, of mythological
figures, nymphs and ivy, azalea-like
florets, and maybe ibises, couple
of those weird Egyptian wading birds, white-
bodied, black-billed, seen in library books.

It is an old bar, an old part of town,
decorated with old, out of place art.
Lyrist with a lyre in a xanthic gown
hangs crooked on one wall. Boy and pacer
on his left; Roman-era habergeon
reflecting light off his chest, the painter

portraying fable, both oafs, travel in

time. James hears that boy's dog and the sheep, *yowl*

and *baa* off the canvas. He sucks oysters,

sips rye, zeroes on the leaning easel.

    He's in the abyss, beyond the pasture's

dense green grass. He once had that shepherd's zeal,

though a herder of Kyloe on cracked land.

One summer their udometer funnel

caught no water. His father said, "God damned

not the land" but him—dead on the Sabbath.

He'd been a tyrant, a czar with no empire,

better zumologist than farmer. *Wrath*

of God real—*hysterical* after

his mother, the men and doctors declared her.

She suffered dysphonia early on.

Later, she'd gyrate in the dead-center

of the kitchen—in her dingy apron,

gab and jabber over that laid Bible.

She'd quote gospel good as any pastor,

Lutheran or other, stand and wabble

hours between meals. Right at three years later

six men carried her away one Sunday.

Eyes on the door, James watches a girl dab
her brow and each pink cheek. Sarah is late.
Stern men in black suits, like those of the mob,
march to the back room. It is a cabal
he knows not to ask the waitress about.
Over that rear door, hanging on the wall,
a fitting scene, surreal, gothic paint:
eyrie, black hawks on a bluff, boy below,
kneeling at a river, fyke in one hand.
Juxtaposition, James mouths. Sundown's glow
falls upon them all, this and that cleft land,
kabook, reddish-brown, sedimentary
stone. *Labefaction*, his next word, next thought,
recalling the brutes, *yahoos*, Swift's story.
He stares at the crack between each rabbet,
split joint of the oak top, the grime and grit
of those who'd writ there before, decades' worth.
    Sailing to Byzantium—he keeps it
folded in his wallet, Yeats' renowned verse.
He feels his age in that oak, in his bones;
his chair the boat, a naomhóg. He hears that tool,

xyster, scraping bone—maybe knife on stone,
grunt in the kitchen, oven hot as hell.

  The etching over fire makes sense; Vulcan,
Roman god hammering out orange metal.
Behind him there is a whack and faint quack.
James turns to find nothing but a closed door.
He pays the tab. Sarah isn't coming back.

  The Wych House has one vacancy, first floor
abuzz. Madam Voilà gives him a fair rate
and breakfast. It's a system, the scrum
on the bottom, soiled paper vulgar men lay
to eat and sleep—for James a new poem.

After Amerigo Vespucci

> I marvel at everything as if it were new.
> —Anna Akhmatova

Assembled in front of the Zenith
we see a coward snipe the President,
blind man belt, "God shed His grace on thee…"
We claim the name—the whole continent.
He nails that poem on the piano.
His big horse-teeth smile shows he knows it.

Little *purple majesties* still grow—
perennial cracked-pot bouquet,
beautiful all fall, *America.*

Beelzebub Pops Out on the Page

The busy bee has no time for sorrow.
—William Blake, *Proverbs of Hell*

Bee, not the queen, just one lone worker
buzzes the wild blue phlox on the bluff.
He's left the swarm and honey for her;
this summer bee, his six weeks of life
to forage & provide. Boyd comes to mind:

> *To be or to do? Which way will you*

go? Drone, the Appalachian kind.

Bittersweet. He has no shoes. Iamb—
her true hum. I'm eternally dumb.

Coming of Age in the Hoosier State

> Come celebrate with me that every day something
> has tried to kill me and has failed.
> —Lucille Clifton, *won't you celebrate with me*

Corn, more than a billion bushels, fields,
thousands of acres, stalks in rows,
columns of buzzcut recruits, jar-heads
of seed—*we, the people*, sow and grow
            in abundance. Off the gravel road
John Deere squats in mud, ungreening, rust
like melanoma. We're always broke.
            We oil our guns & knives. Spit-shine our black
boots. Stand tall. Fall for *the republic.*

D.H. Lawrence Stories Line the Top Shelf

> I was standing in the most absolute aloneness that
> I had ever been given.
>
> —James Dickey, *Deliverance*

Deciduous, black & white oaks, maples,
red and sugar, shed their golden robes
Dahlonega to Underwood. Bells,
cross-topped spires, white gables, copper domes
gleam in fractured orange rays. Autumn
demands her own appliqué quilt. Home's
this mountain; it hibernates till rain
bares her crooked spine. I trek this land—
odor of chrysanthemums downwind.

Elementary Calculations

Everyone gets the experience. Some get the lesson.
—T. S. Eliot

E uclid, *father of geometry*,
multiplied my troubles in high school.
Those test scores were proof enough to see
I would fail. See, I studied each girl—
         her parabolas, curves of her eye-
brows, cheeks, lips, chin, breasts, hips, and derrière.
It was step by step, logical, why
there—plus French, shape of a pêche, along
with how I wronged them with my tongue.

Flocks Hide the Weak and the Humble Strong

> For to be social is to be forgiving.
> —Robert Frost, *The Star-splitter*

Forgiveness, attribute of the *strong*,
    Gandi penned. I surf for the right word:
effete, feeble, frail, unfit, weakling—
    one fitting antonym. A hurt bird
flits in circles around an oak leaf,
    one wing kicking up dust, determined
to fly. It's not fleeing the sunned bluff,
stone—the boy with the slingshot. The wind
whispers coolly, *One breath frees the self.*

Gallivanting Bookstore to Bookstore

> I'm half living my life between reality and fantasy at
> all times.
>
> —Lady Gaga

Gutenberg gives the masses the first
printed Bible. Genesis. Voices
become ravens; they travel like Christ.
Gospel: He went to Gethsemane—
the garden. We know the very spot,
near the Mount, place of arrest, being
carried off. I read Glück: "I don't want
to be burned." Seeing is believing.
She's reading Yeats, *The Second Coming*.

Hard-Faced and Callused They Came in Hordes

> The way we are living, timorous or bold, will have
> been our life.
>> —Seamus Heaney, *Elegy*

onyocks, dad called us. We didn't get
the derogatory one, *hunyaks*—
for immigrants, people of the dirt.
Our people. The past. They broke their backs
over the hardscrabble land, for corn
for the heifers and hogs, the next wish.

Dad sold guns. Mom bought our food; frozen
ground beef, pork fritters, ice cream, and square fish.
In one generation—*Grow* from *Groh*.

Inside the Book I Am Merely Ink

> Nothing helps a man to reform like thinking of the
> past with regret.
>
> —Fyodor Dostoyevsky, *The Idiot*

I the ninth letter, the first Roman
numeral, very first character.
Fyodor Dostoyevsky: "I am
a sick man... I think my liver
is diseased." *Indianapolis*—

one home I don't put in a poem.
Aren't we all the *indigenous*?
Womb invaders? The blink of an eye?
The Idiot? *Woe is me*—not *I*.

Juice and Mogen David on Sundays

> Men screamed, the bugles screamed, walls broke in
> the air/We never knew till then that He was there.
> —Robinson Jeffers, *The Truce and the Peace*

Jesus is in the juice. That's Baptist.
Lutherans use wine—consecrated
like the hard white bread. The eucharist:
first over the crypt of King David.

We're told Grace made wine from concord grapes.
We witnessed clusters every summer.

They hung on. The dog ate them in place.
Buzzing stingers came for their sugar—
ovipositors shape of a *J*.

Kavanagh Comes to Mind Days Like This

> On the stem of memory imaginations blossom.
> —Patrick Kavanagh, *Through the Open Door*

Kentucky River zigzagging west
under us, wheeling even farther
south, toward Knoxville, the oaks undress
in the rain, leave their autumn attire
on the yellow lines and broken white
one kestrel straddles, fawn, cadaver—
one of the herd, dinner for the flight.

We picnic roadside, talk, point out black
clouds, twine—red kite flapping in the oak.

Lions in the Wake of the Last Storm

> I didn't come for answers
> to a place like this, I came to walk
> on the earth, still cold, still silent.
> —Philip Levine, *Gospel*

Lion crouched in the savanna

grass, mane sunlit-silver, eyes zeroed

like spotter and sniper scopes, Georgia

zoo-goers line the wire licking ice cream.

My dad would call this *lollygagging*.

Alphas peer at each other; Marine

and lion. One dreams of attacking.

One walking. "Denied his pride, sawt, soul—

he's more lethal," he growls to the girl.

Myopic, One of Two, Minimum

> You see, I am a poet, and not quite right in the
> head, darling. It's only that.
> —Edna St. Vincent Millay

Michaelangelo, man and marble
statue, *David*, seventeen feet tall—
Renaissance art, called *monumental*.

We reduce mountains to men, chisel
away layers only time creates.

I must see that Tuscany quarry,
the pit men climb out of—place of grace
surely. She looks up momentarily.

"I thought he'd be bigger. Such the dream."

Narcissus Kneels at Standing Water

> Let us forget with generosity those who cannot
> love us.
> > —Pablo Neruda, *Sonata with Some Pine Trees*

Nymphs thread a halo, gold in the sun—
clouds swarm over his colossal head.

Echo ricochets off the mountain,

river a green pool, larvae, eggs laid—

wriggler to mosquito. *Little fly*,

a Spanish girl says. "One to zillions.

He loved no one, but... He chose to die."

Two disembodied voices remain.

In nectar & blood we kneel to listen.

From the Caravaggio painting, Narcissus (1599)

October That River's Bronze Olive

> There is a strange edge to the wind today.
> —John O'Donohue, *The Transparent Border*

Out of school, home, we call them to come
'round the ottoman, like a lone scow
we'll tow up the river we can't plumb.
Fall's not bled the Okefenokee.
Halloween will reek of pumpkin rot;
that starved flesh folds in its own gangrene.

Plots of corn anchor in the north bank,
stalks like dug-in grunts in dungarees—
dusk a blood stripe, one *gung-ho* echo.

In memory of John R. DeMoss (USMC, 1968-69)

Pigeons Would Be Pigs If Not for Wings

> I have suffered the atrocity of sunsets.
> —Sylvia Plath, *Elm*

Pigs! We smelt them on South West 60
   about 300 South, August air
sweltering, the cab of that Chevy
a shut corn crib we'd come to suffer—
rusted bed of apples in barrels,
raked up off baked ground, rotten or not.

The neighbor's kin raised pigs. Flocked grackles
watched us dump them in mud, feed the lot.
Baffling... All that fruit and still that fat.
   I knew their fate. I named one, *pork chop*.

Questions Not Asked about the Future

> We do not learn first what to talk about and then
> what to say about it.
>
> —Willard Van Orman Quine

Quiet Riot, *Cum on Feel the Noize*,
1983, first rock album.
We wore out that vinyl on Billy's
RCA—and that *taupe* carpet in our room.

Hard to believe brown was ever *in*—
but I don't recall us protesting.
　　　Queensrÿche, *Silent Lucidity*, when
"It was all a bad dream spinning…"
　　　Jeezus! We didn't see this coming!

Rabbit Holes Every Verse and Last Word

> Winning does not tempt that man.
> This is how he grows: by being defeated, decisively,
> by constantly greater beings.
> —Rainer Maria Rilke, *The Man Watching*

R abbits colonized the entire farm.
  We found footprints, white cotton fibers

along the barbed wire, among the corn

stalks, burrow holes, brush piles, and briars.

"It's like shooting fish in a barrel,"

dad said. Rain flooded every acre.

We'd been called there to *dispatch* them, deal

with the thieves, save nature from nature.

  I'd read Genesis. It wasn't *murder*.

Stand, Count Them, Those of the Republic

> They forgot where they came from. They lost sight
> of what brought them along.
>
> —Carl Sandburg

Standing in the stadium, Roman-
like, those who waited for the Christians, words,
release of the lions, the human
carnage, the slaughter, then swooping birds.
     Bit more civil today, Saturday—
and some kneeling during the anthem,
some mad chucking stones, cities ablaze.
     I salute the ones some hate—women,
men, praying, readying at the gates.

The Baptist Loved God Despite the Slight

> Always there is something more to know.
> —Natasha Trethewey, *Monument*

Tchaikovsky streaming, Trethewey laid
out on ringed cherry, my mind's on swans—
trumpeters, those white-bodied, black-faced
wintering in the delta. Back then
men told women to fear God and *shush*.

     The old Baptist told her granddaughters
she'd named them: Trish, Tria, Trista. Pens—
those girls swam Mississippi's waters.

     In *The Trinity*, they are absent.

Under Gray They Stir and Wake Unplugged

> Poetry is the power of defining the indefinable in
> terms of the unforgettable.
> —Louis Untermeyer, *The Pursuit of Poetry*

U ptown, we coffee at the cafe.
   Atop Walgreens, they stoop pallbearer-
still, black eyes dialed into the grave.
      Not unique to our species or theirs.
The couple left of us, from Brazil,
spots them, too, and the bloated dumpster
behind BK. Buzzards *wake* to that smell.
Offal river in wind, it leaks through.
The unplugged one points and says, *Urubú.*

"Violet, Not Violent!," She Wrote

> The world's perverse, but it could be worse.
> —Mona Van Duyn, *Sonnet for Minimalists*

Vase of viola sororia—
even more viola pedata.
A fifty-percent chance of showers?
   Outdoors, agalinis purpurea
in the grass and tradescantia
ohiensis, blue-violet flowers
along managed stones and drooped foxglove.
Gaia's wet and purple. It poured hours.
   Some man named her child, *Roy G. Biv.*

What's the Word for Hoosiers Who Have Fled?

> Do I contradict myself? Very well, then I
> contradict myself, I am large, I contain multitudes.
> —Walt Whitman, *Song of Myself*

Willow between the fence and window
       we kept ourselves from the ugliness.
It was "the presidential palace,"
       the sheriff said—along the Dnipro,
though he used a different third-world
ditch. I might've mentioned Chicago
       but that's a wide net. See, I've emerged
from that white house, beyond the willow,
fields, cricks, through rich peat, from seed you sow.

Xylobium Orchids Lined Her Sill

> People don't realize how a man's whole life can be
> changed by one book.
>> —Malcolm X, *The Autobiography of Malcolm X*

X—bit more than one man's signature
seen in the county clerk's musty books,

examining marriage logs I pour

over for proof in the crooks and hooks—

some government man's seal and *I swear*

in iron gall ink, oxidized blur,

intersecting slashes, purple & black marks.

He was an illiterate *farmer*

She—*homemaker*—another man's *X*.

Yew Over the Laughery Valley

> Everything we look upon is blest.
> —W.B. Yeats, *A Dialogue of Self and Soul*

Yellowjackets, those ground-nesters, rose
from one rodent burrow on the slope.
One stung me twice and went on buzzing.

I trekked on uphill, acorns crunching
under my boots. It was copper, thin,
green-needled, arils scarlet in sun—
autumn on the crest and in the wind.
Little grows in that sandstone and clay.

What's killed men jays ate in day's last ray.

Zero to Sixty in Eight Seconds

> Only emotion objectified endures.
> —Louis Zukofsky, *A Test of Poetry*

*Z*ero and *Big Red* between my thighs
I crank up ZZ Top. *Velcro Fly*. Green,
first gear, I go easy through the light.

To be seen and heard. I'm seventeen.
Zealous. Top down, I zoom up Lincoln.
The man who'll buy this car in nine months

will die in a crash. I smell chicken—
pan-fried, and the *King's* pizza. And gas.
Those girls. It was all one rush and buzz.

*　　*　　*

What can be explained is not poetry.

—William Butler Yeats

Author's Note

First, thank you for the gift of your time. Even reading this note is appreciated. If you read these poems, you certainly figured out I used each letter in the alphabet to start each poem. And, except for the first poem, I ended each poem with the same letter. And, each title starts with that letter, as does the last name of the poet, philosopher, or artist credited in the epigraph. With rare exception, like the first, each poem is nine lines, and each line is nine syllables, including each poem title. (Plus, I like the ninth letter of the alphabet.) Why write in iambic pentameter? Or any other traditional form? Because a poem must have meaning and melody, I used many traditional poetry devices (alliteration, assonance, consonance, simile, metaphor, imagery, rhyming, etc.). Most end rhymes, you might have noticed, are slant rhymes. Nothing in this collection was forced. So, if you read that, I failed as a writer.

Last, I wanted to express a sense of community in this collection. You should've noticed many collective nouns, like "pride" and "sawt" in *Lions in the Wake of the Last Storm*, and "colonized" in *Rabbit Holes Every Verse and Last Word*. Even when we move into another's space we tend to move in like masses. This is not unique to our species. But that's for another collection.

Robert E. Ray
September 2025
Georgia, U.S.A.

P.S. I hope you laughed, too. We should make room for humor, especially in poetry.

Credits

I've read hundreds of poems over the past nine years.
That's when I started writing poetry. I undoubtedly leak
some of those influences in my own writing. Constantly
mindful of that possibility, I'm diligent reviewing what I
write to ensure it's my own work. Still, I must say the Irish
poets, particularly William Butler Yeats, Patrick Kavanagh,
and Seamus Heaney have influenced much of my poetry.

Many key words in the first poem, *The Scrum*, came from
White's Modern Dictionary of The English Language, published
in 1905. I have that hardback edition in my office and use
it often. Those words and definitions reflect a different era.
It's your call whether they fit today.

Robert E. Ray's poetry has been published by Rattle, The Ekphrastic Review, Wild Roof Journal, The Wee Sparrow Poetry Press, The Nuthatch, The Muleskinner Journal, Beyond Words Literary Magazine, and numerous print and digital anthologies. He is a graduate of Eastern Kentucky University. Robert lives in rural southeast Georgia.

"Where memory, myth, and melody meet—the alphabet comes alive in verse."

"A journey through America and beyond, one letter—and one poem—at a time."

"Poetry that hums with humor, history, and the heartbeat of belonging."

"From cornfields to cathedrals, a buzzing celebration of language and life."

"Twenty-six poems, countless echoes—*Abuzz* is language alive with grace."

"Poetry that crackles with history, humor, and heart."

"An American story told A to Z—in verse."

"Sharp, musical, and alive—poems that stick with you."

"Where tradition meets edge: poetry buzzing with life."

www.ingramcontent.com/pod-product-compliance
Lightning Source LLC
Chambersburg PA
CBHW031635040426
42452CB00007B/844